Gemstones have been a source of delight and fascination for many thousands of years. The first section of this book explores the nature of gemstones and their special attributes of beauty, rarity and durability. The mineral properties which govern these qualities and provide a means of identifying gems are described and illustrated. The section ends with a brief account of gem cutting.

The most popular gemstones are described in the central section of the book, along with many less well-known but equally beautiful gems. Some common imitations and synthetics are also described, with illustrations of the different internal 'landscapes' found in these and natural gemstones.

The final section of the book is concerned with how gem minerals form, where they are found and how they are mined. There is also a short section on how gems are identified, and a selected index to the main gem species, technical terms and important topics such as colour.

The authors have the good fortune to work with one of the world's finest public collections of gemstones, which is displayed in the Gemstones Exhibition at the Geological Museum in London. The collection consists of gem minerals in both a natural state and cut as exquisite gemstones, and has its origins in the specimens brought together by the British Geological Survey from 1835 onwards to illustrate 'the applications of geology to the useful purposes of life'. A selection of outstanding items in the exhibition is shown on this page and opposite.

In 1985 the Geological Museum was merged with the British Museum (Natural History) which possesses one of the finest mineral collections in the world. Most of the photographs in this book were commissioned specially and feature many gems displayed in the Geological Museum, as well as some of the fine crystals and cut gems on view in the Mineral Gallery of the British Museum (Natural History).

Large spodumene crystal and cut gemstone from Brazil.

1

GEMSTONES IN HISTORY

1 Sumerian court jewellery from Ur, set with lapis lazuli and cornelian

The desire for jewellery and beautiful objects is one that we share with our earliest ancestors. Our rings, lucky charms and royal regalia reflect a tradition of self-adornment, magic and ritual which extends back many thousands of years.

The oldest jewellery comes from graves perhaps 20 000 years old, and consists of shell, bone and ivory 'necklaces'. We do not know what significance these objects held for their owners but in later ages gemstones have been used as symbols of divine and earthly power, to display wealth and status, and to protect the wearer from the many misfortunes encountered in an uncertain world.

The beauty and desirability of gold and precious stones inspired an early flowering of the decorative arts. Jade carving was already established in China 4500 years ago, and at the same time Sumerian and Egyptian craftsmen were fashioning intricate jewellery set with lapis lazuli, cornelian, turquoise, amethyst and garnet (fig 1). Agates held a

2 Cameo of the Emperor Augustus, first century AD

special fascination for the Romans, whose skill in exploiting the differently coloured layers produced cameos of unsurpassed beauty. These cameos were prized and some were embellished long after the fall of Rome. The diadem of the Augustus cameo (fig 2) was added in medieval times.

Where did these gemstones come from? Beautifully coloured pebbles in stream beds and on beaches were probably the first gems to attract the human eye and imagination. As civilisations evolved, a greater variety of gem minerals and more reliable sources of supply became available through organised mining and trading. The Egyptians mined turquoise in Sinai and amethyst near Aswan but they imported lapis lazuli from Badakhshan in Afghanistan, the only source known to the ancient world. These remote mines are perhaps the world's longest operating mines, still yielding the finest quality lapis lazuli after more than 6000 years. The Romans mined much agate near Idar-Oberstein in Germany

and, after centuries of neglect, these deposits again formed the basis of a thriving local industry from medieval times.

The gem gravels of India, Sri Lanka and Burma are legendary for the rich variety of their gemstones, producing the finest diamonds, sapphires, rubies and spinels for many centuries. An ancient Sanskrit manuscript records that Indian diamonds were an important source of state revenue over 2000 years ago.

The great gems from these sources have always exerted a powerful fascination. Some have retained an individual identity through many colourful adventures, acquiring a charisma beyond ordinary commercial values. When the Koh-i-Noor diamond was presented to the Mughal Emperor Babur in 1526, its value was set at 'one day of the whole world's expenditure'. A few of these gems even carry written evidence of an illustrious past, as on the Shah Diamond (fig 3) which is inscribed with the names of three royal owners including that of Shah Jahan.

Exquisite gems have come from more recently discovered deposits in the Americas, Africa, Australia and Siberia. Magnificent Colombian emeralds first reached Europe in the sixteenth century, in the plunder of the Conquistadors. They surpassed in colour and size those previously mined in Habachtal and Egypt (fig 4). Exploration of Brazil has revealed gem deposits especially rich in topaz, tourmaline, chrysoberyl and agates. South African diamonds and Australian opals are two important nineteenth century discoveries. This century has seen the expansion of the diamond industry into Siberia, Australia and many African countries. Newly discovered minerals and mineral varieties, such as charoite and tanzanite, have increased the range of materials available to jewellers, but the functions of our jewellery remain the same as those so important to our ancestors – to beautify and to impress.

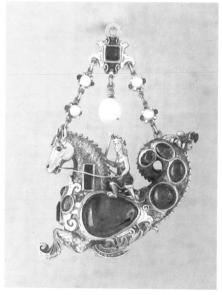

4 Spanish Renaissance pendant set with Colombian emeralds

3 The Shah Diamond

5 Sapphires and diamonds in modern jewellery.

WHAT ARE GEMSTONES?

From ancient times many materials, natural and artificial, have been set in jewellery and other precious objects. Over the centuries however, the term gemstone has come to mean a naturally occurring mineral desirable for its beauty, valuable in its rarity and sufficiently durable to give lasting pleasure.

Most gemstones are minerals that have formed in a variety of environments within the Earth. Minerals have a definite chemical composition and ordered atomic arrangement so that their physical and optical properties are constant or vary only within narrow limits. These properties, such as density and refraction, can be measured accurately and are used to identify a mineral.

Ideally gemstones should be hard and unaffected by the temperatures, pressures, abrasive dusts and chemicals encountered in our everyday lives. The majority are silicates and include emerald, aquamarine, peridot and amethyst, as well as many exotic rarities. Ruby, sapphire, spinel and chrysoberyl are oxides. Diamond is unique among gems in being composed of a single chemical element – carbon. Nephrite, jadeite and lapis lazuli are rocks, that is, aggregates of one or more minerals.

Plants and animals are the sources of the more fragile 'organic' gems that have been used for ornament since very ancient times. Jet and amber are the fossilised wood and resin of extinct trees, while pearls, shells and most corals are calcium carbonate structures formed by aquatic animals. Ivories are the tusks and teeth of land and sea mammals.

8 Orange sapphire

6 Helmet shell cameo

7 Diamond crystal in kimberlite

9 A large cut citrine

Gems display an almost limitless variety in their beauty. Qualities as diverse as the fiery brilliance of diamond and the soft iridescence of pearl, the bold patterns of agate and pale translucency of jade inspire our admiration and fascination.

Light is the source of all beauty in gemstones. Interactions between minerals and light cause the intense colours of ruby and lapis lazuli, the sparkling fire of diamond and the play of rainbow colours in opal. Light reflected at the surface gives each gem a distinctive lustre which may have the brilliance of diamond or the subtlety of jade, and light scattered and reflected from the gem's interior causes the soft glow in moonstone.

Fine colour combined with flawless transparency is the ideal of beauty in many gem species. Mineral inclusions, however, form the chief attraction in some gems, causing the colour spangling in aventurine quartz and sunstone, and reflecting the cat's-eyes and stars that gleam from some chrysoberyls and sapphires.

The attraction of the more subtly coloured agates and jaspers lies in the enormous variety of patterns and textures that develop as these minerals grow, the growth bands and trapped mineral fragments often resembling exotic landscapes and gardens.

Most gemstones show little beauty in the rough state: their full colour and lustre is revealed only by skilled cutting and polishing. Diamond's magnificent fire is displayed best in the most precisely cut and well proportioned of stones.

When we wear jewellery our movements create a continuously changing relationship between the gemstones and the light falling on them, adding sparkle to their colour and fire. Spotlights enhance the 'life' of diamonds, rubies and emeralds, while soft lighting brings out the glow of amber and pearls.

RARITY

If beauty creates the initial impact of gemstones then rarity imparts an aura of exclusiveness and worth that increases our desire to possess them. Rarity determines the fabulous values placed on the great gems of the world and is a major influence on the prices of the gems displayed in every jeweller's shop window.

Gems may be rare in one or more respects. Many gems are varieties of common materials, their rarity residing in an exceptional colour or clarity. Quartz and feldspars together make up about two-thirds of the Earth's crust but most are grey or cream. Very little quartz has the beautiful colour and flawless transparency of a fine amethyst, and only rarely does labradorite feldspar display a rainbow iridescence (fig 11). A few gem minerals are of rare occurrence: diamond forms a minute proportion of the kimberlite host rock – about 5 grams in 100 tonnes. Other minerals contain rare chemical elements such as the beryllium in taaffeite and emerald (fig 12).

In a few exceptional gems these qualities are combined with uncommonly large size: the Cullinan diamond weighed 3106 carats in its rough state. Cullinan I (fig 10) weighs 530·20 carats and is the largest cut diamond of fine colour in the world.

The commercial value of a gemstone depends on the quality of colour, freedom from internal flaws and weight. The weight of a gem is measured in *carats* (5 carats = 1 gram), and gems are usually sold by weight at so much per carat. The density of gem minerals varies so that a yellow sapphire will appear smaller than a less dense citrine of similar weight. Gem density is measured as the *specific gravity*, by comparing the weight of the gem with the weight of an equal volume of water.

Gem values, like ideals of beauty, vary with fashions and beliefs in different cultures, fluctuating with public demand and the availability of a particular gem.

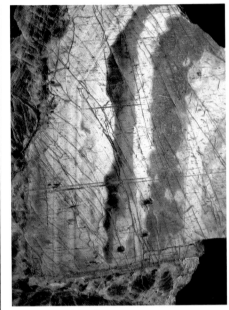

11 Iridescent labradorite

10 The Great Star of Africa (Cullinan I), set in the Sceptre with the Cross, British Crown Jewels

12 Taaffeite

Gems endure through time because they are resistant to chemical alteration, are sufficiently hard to retain a good polish and are not easily chipped or broken.

Hardness is the measure of a gemstone's resistance to abrasion. The most easily and commonly used standard is Mohs' scale of hardness, which was set up in 1822 by the German mineralogist Friedrich Mohs. Mohs selected 10 well-known minerals and numbered them in order of scratch hardness, such that a mineral will scratch all minerals having a lower hardness number. The complete scale, in order of increasing hardness, is talc (1), gypsum (2), calcite (3), fluorite (4), apatite (5), orthoclase feldspar (6), quartz (7), topaz (8), corundum (9) and diamond (10).

Almost all dust and grit in the atmosphere consists of quartz, which is number 7 on Mohs' scale, so that a gem should have a hardness of 7 or more if it is to retain a good polish.

The intervals between Mohs numbers do not represent equal increases in hardness, the difference in hardness between diamond and corundum being far greater than that between corundum and talc. A truer comparison is given by indentation tests, such as the Knoop Test (fig 13), where dents produced by a diamond point at controlled pressures are measured. Such tests, however, require complex instruments.

To wear well, a gemstone must also be tough. Despite being harder than quartz, emerald and zircon are brittle and chip easily, and diamond and topaz are among the many gems that may cleave along planes of weak atomic bonding if dropped or knocked against hard objects (fig 15). The toughest gems are jadeite, nephrite and agate, all of which have a hardness of 7 or less. Their strength derives from their structure which consists of a mass of minute, interlocking fibres or grains and permits them to be fashioned into the most exquisite bowls and intricate carvings (fig 14).

15 Cleavages in a diamond crystal

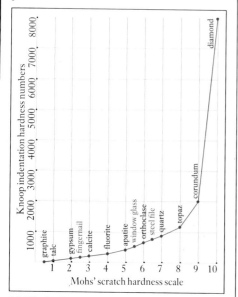

13 The Mohs and Knoop hardness scales

14 Delicate nephrite bowl and nephrite structure (inset) magnified ×35

CRYSTAL STRUCTURE

Beautifully formed crystals are an outward expression of the orderly atomic structure that exists in most minerals. Ideally, crystalline substances are built of units identical in shape, size and chemical composition, the shape of these basic units controlling the symmetry and overall shape of the crystals. A mineral crystallises in one of seven symmetry *systems*, examples of which are shown in fig 16. In nature, growth conditions are seldom ideal so that structural defects and chemical impurities occur in almost all minerals. However, all crystalline minerals possess an orderly atomic structure whether they form as outwardly shapeless masses or are found as waterworn pebbles.

Crystal structure influences many mineral properties that are important in cutting and identifying gemstones (fig 17). For example, atoms may be less strongly bonded in some crystal planes, giving rise to directions of easy breaking or *cleavage*. Hardness may also vary with crystal direction. Crystal structure affects the way in which light travels through a substance. In all minerals, other than cubic and non-crystalline minerals, light is split into two rays that travel at different speeds and along different paths through the crystal structure. In coloured minerals the rays may be differently absorbed within the structure and emerge as two or three different colours or shades of the same colour. This effect is called *pleochroism* and causes the directional variations in colour seen in many gem minerals.

17 The crystalline structure of kunzite

Kunzite is pleochroic: the deepest colour is seen if one looks at the crystal end on. Gems cut with the table facet at right angles to the length of the crystal display the best colour. Kunzite appears almost colourless across the crystal length.

Kunzite is composed of chains of silicon and oxygen atoms which are linked by lithium and aluminium atoms sited between the chains. This structure is shown magnified many million times.

Kunzite cleaves easily in two directions, along planes of weak atomic bonding between the silicon-oxygen chains.

Kunzite crystals are rarely as perfectly formed as the crystal shown in the main drawing.

Irregular termination and faces.

Broken surface where the crystal was attached to the host rock.

CUBIC
diamond, garnet

TETRAGONAL
zircon

HEXAGONAL
emerald, aquamarine

TRIGONAL
ruby, sapphire

ORTHORHOMBIC
peridot

MONOCLINIC
orthoclase

TRICLINIC
axinite

16 The seven crystal symmetry systems

Each gem mineral interacts with light in constant and measurable ways, and these properties can be used in its identification.

Light entering a mineral is slowed down and refracted (bent) from its original path in air (fig 18). Cubic and non-crystalline minerals are *singly refractive,* meaning that light is slowed and refracted equally in all directions through the mineral. Minerals crystallising in all other systems are *doubly refractive:* the light entering is split into two rays that are differently slowed and refracted, and which travel along different paths through the crystal structure. Double images may be seen through minerals, such as the calcite in fig 19, where these differences are large.

A constant mathematical relationship, called the *refractive index,* exists between the angle at which light strikes a mineral and the angle of refraction. Singly refractive minerals have only one refractive index. Doubly refractive minerals show a range of refractive indices between an upper and lower limit characteristic of each mineral; the numerical difference between the maximum and minimum indices is called the *birefringence.*

The term *lustre* describes the amount of light reflected from the surface of a gem or mineral. Diamond shows a very high lustre which is described as adamantine. Most gems have a glassy lustre while less lustrous surfaces, such as those of turquoise, nephrite and amber, are variously described as waxy, greasy and resinous.

Beautiful effects are caused by the reflection of light from mineral inclusions and structures within some gems. Cat's-eyes (fig 21) and stars (fig 44) are reflected from one or several sets of fine, parallel fibres or tubes that have developed in certain crystal directions.

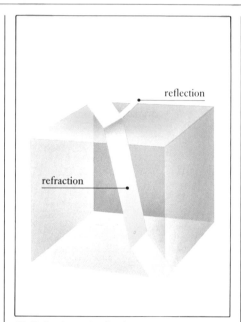

18 Reflection and refraction

20 The lustre of zircon

19 Double refraction in calcite

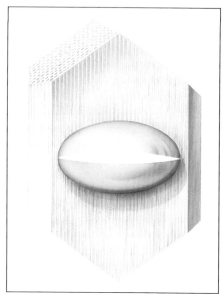

21 Cat's-eye effect in chrysoberyl

COLOUR

Many gems appear coloured because part of the white light travelling through them is absorbed within the mineral structure. White light is a mixture of many colours (page 11) but only when one or more of these colours is removed does the light emerging from a gem appear coloured. The causes of absorption are complex, generally involving the presence of particular chemical elements and damage or irregularities in the crystal structure.

Most gems are coloured by a limited range of metals, the most important of which are chromium, iron, manganese, titanium, and copper. Chromium gives the intense red of ruby and brilliant greens of emerald and demantoid garnet, while iron causes the more subtle reds, blues, greens and yellows in almandine garnet, spinels, sapphires, peridots and chrysoberyls. The most prized blue sapphires are coloured by titanium with iron. Copper gives the blues and greens of turquoise and malachite, manganese the pink of rhodonite and orange of spessartine garnet.

In most gems these metallic elements occur as impurities, usually in minute amounts. Such gems can show a wide range of different colours (fig 22), and because they contain such small amounts of impurity the colour of some may be altered, enhanced or destroyed by heating or by irradiation with gamma rays and X-rays.

In a few gems the colouring elements form an essential part of the chemical composition, for example the copper in turquoise, manganese in rhodonite, and iron in peridot and almandine garnet. These gems have a very limited colour range, generally restricted to shades of one colour (fig 23). Such colours are very stable and impossible to alter greatly without destroying the mineral.

22 Sapphires and rubies coloured by traces of metallic impurities

23 Turquoise

The brilliant colours displayed by opal and labradorite, and in the fiery sparkle of diamonds, arise when white light is split into its constituent colours. White light consists of electromagnetic waves of different wavelengths, each wavelength appearing a particular colour. A complete 'rainbow' spectrum exists, from the long red through to the shorter violet wavelengths.

Dispersion is the origin of the 'fire' in gemstones. When light enters a mineral the various wavelengths are differently refracted, red the least and violet the most, so that the colour spectrum is spread out (fig 24). Gem minerals vary greatly in their ability to disperse light, and their dispersion can be measured as the numerical difference between the refractive indices of specific blue and red wavelengths.

Interference causes the iridescence in labradorite and the rainbow effects seen in cleavage cracks and on tarnished surfaces. When light falls on very thin, transparent mineral layers, as in labradorite, it is reflected from both the upper and lower surfaces (fig 24). Since the reflected rays have travelled different distances the wave troughs and peaks of the various wavelengths either coincide or are out of step. A colour is enhanced if they coincide but little or no colour is seen for out-of-step wavelengths.

In precious opal, which is composed of transparent, regularly sized and stacked spheres, light is scattered by the network of voids between the spheres (fig 26). Interference occurs between the emerging rays, the range of colours seen depending on the size of the spheres and the angle at which the opal is viewed. Larger spheres produce a complete spectrum as the opal is tilted, but small spheres generate only blues and violets.

25 Dispersion in the Cullinan II diamond

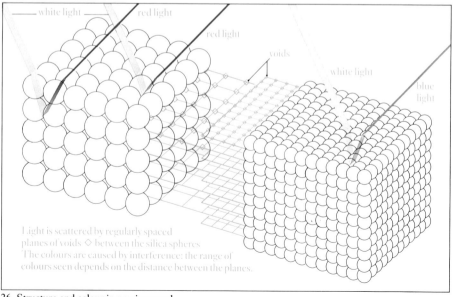

Light is scattered by regularly spaced planes of voids ◇ between the silica spheres. The colours are caused by interference: the range of colours seen depends on the distance between the planes.

26 Structure and colour in precious opal

27 Play of colour in opal

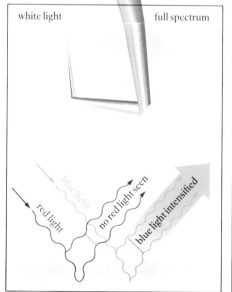

white light   full spectrum

blue light   no red light seen   red light   blue light intensified   red light

24 Dispersion (above) and interference

CUTTING & POLISHING

A skilled lapidary can turn a rough pebble into a sparkling and valuable gemstone. The knowledge needed for this transformation has been built up over many centuries, and today a style of cutting can be selected to display the special qualities of every gem.

When deciding how best to cut a gemstone, the lapidary must consider the shape of the rough material and the position of flaws, such as fractures and inclusions. He must also be aware of the mineral's optical properties and cleavages: it is difficult to produce a good polish parallel to cleavage directions and pleochroic gems should be oriented to show their best colour. However, the cut is often a compromise between displaying the full beauty of a mineral and producing the biggest gemstone possible, since size also affects the value.

Cabochons are the oldest, simplest cuts, being round or oval gems with plain, curved surfaces. Still in use today, cabochons display best the colours and patterns in opaque and translucent stones, and optical effects such as sheen, iridescence, cat's-eyes and stars.

The faceted styles now used for almost all transparent gems developed much later, becoming important in medieval Europe. In these styles the surface of the gem is worked into a pattern of highly polished, flat planes which act as mirrors. Some light is reflected from the surface of the crown (top) facets, displaying the lustre; light entering the gem is reflected back through the top of the stone from the pavilion (bottom) facets, displaying the colour and fire. The facets must be precisely angled to bring out the maximum beauty, the angles varying according to the optical properties of each gem mineral. In badly cut stones light leaks out through the pavilion so that colour and fire are lost.

The brilliant and step cuts are the most familiar styles in modern western jewellery. The brilliant cut was developed to show off the superb lustre and fire of diamond, but is also used for many other gems. Step cuts are most effective in stones such as emeralds and rubies, where colour is the supreme quality.

29 A superbly cut citrine and a poorly cut sapphire

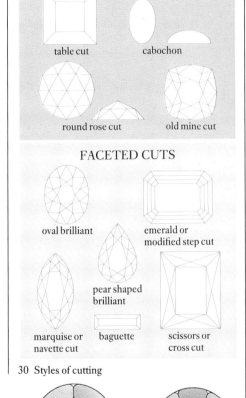

OLD CUTS

table cut   cabochon

round rose cut   old mine cut

FACETED CUTS

oval brilliant   emerald or modified step cut

pear shaped brilliant

marquise or navette cut   baguette   scissors or cross cut

30 Styles of cutting

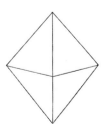

a Rough octahedral crystal

b Crystal is sawn

c Sawn crystal is rounded

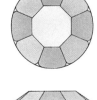

d, e, f Table (orange), bezel facets (pink) and pavilion main facets (blue) are ground and polished. The pavilion point is ground flat to form a culet.

28 Stages in producing a brilliant-cut diamond

31 Marking a diamond crystal for cutting

32 Sawing a diamond crystal

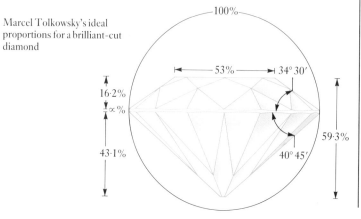

33 Diamonds are faceted on a revolving scaife (wheel)

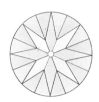

g Star facets are added to the crown

h Upper girdle facets complete the crown

i Lower girdle facets complete the pavilion

Marcel Tolkowsky's ideal proportions for a brilliant-cut diamond

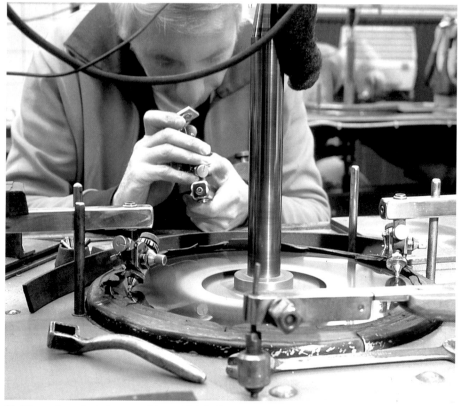

100%

53%   34° 30'

16·2%
∝ %
43·1%

59·3%

40° 45'

DIAMOND

Diamond is named from the Greek 'adamas', meaning unconquerable, an early recognition that it is the hardest of all natural minerals. This supreme hardness is combined with exceptional lustre and dispersion, giving diamond the lasting fiery brilliance for which it is prized.

It is perhaps difficult to believe that diamond, like graphite and charcoal, is a form of carbon. Diamond crystallises in the cubic system, at enormous pressures and high temperatures. Its exceptional properties arise from the crystal structure, in which the bonding between the carbon atoms is immensely strong and uniform. Much diamond occurs as well-formed crystals (fig 35), most commonly as octahedra (fig 36). Graphite, which has a hardness of 1 to 2 on Mohs' scale, consists of weakly bonded sheets of carbon atoms. Charcoal is non-crystalline.

Diamond is the most intensively mined and carefully graded of all gem minerals. The quality of a gem diamond is assessed by a system popularly summarised as the 'Four Cs': colour, clarity, cut and carat weight.

Diamond varies from colourless, through a range of yellows and browns, to green, blue, pink and a very rare red. Colourless diamonds or those of strong or unusual colour are considered the most valuable. Truly colourless stones are rare: most diamonds are tinged with yellow or brown. These colours are due to impurities, the most common being nitrogen. Depending on the amount present and its distribution in the crystal structure, nitrogen gives rise to browns, yellows, greens and black. Blue diamonds contain minute traces of boron.

Clarity is judged on the extent of mineral inclusions and flaws, such as cleavages, visible at ×10 magnification. Although inclusions may devalue gemstones commercially, they may also provide valuable information about the origin of a mineral. Studies of some garnet and pyroxene inclusions, coupled with a knowledge of the conditions needed to

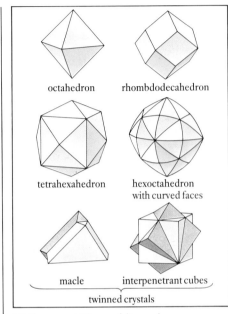

octahedron rhombdodecahedron

tetrahexahedron hexoctahedron with curved faces

macle interpenetrant cubes

twinned crystals

35 Some crystal forms of diamond

34 Diamond crystals on a slab of jet

36 Octahedral diamond crystal.

37 Diamond crystals in kimberlite from Kimberley, South Africa (top right), and Siberia (centre), and in a beach conglomerate from Namaqualand (top left)

DIAMOND

synthesise diamond, reveal that diamonds formed at depths of 100 to 200 km.

The cut is of supreme importance in displaying the full beauty of diamond. Although diamonds were known in India 2300 years ago, crystals were not cut for many centuries because it was believed that this would destroy the supposed magical properties of diamond. In Europe, the polishing of simple point and table cuts from octahedral crystals, and rose cuts from cleavage fragments, began sometime after 1300. The popularity of diamond has grown with the development of the brilliant cut, which best displays the fire in diamond. Although early versions appeared in the seventeenth century, the modern form of this cut was set in 1919, when Marcel Tolkowsky published the ideal dimensions for a brilliant-cut diamond (fig 28).

Diamond is ground and polished with powdered diamond; this is only possible because diamond is less hard in certain crystal directions. Diamond also cleaves relatively easily, in four directions parallel to the octahedral crystal faces. Cleaving is sometimes used to divide large crystals and to trim away flawed material.

For over 2000 years, diamonds were found only as eroded crystals in river gravels. Until 1725 India was the major source of diamonds, with much smaller amounts mined in Kalimantan (Borneo). Diamonds were then discovered in Brazil, which became the leading supplier as Indian production waned. South African diamonds were found first in 1867, in gravels near the Orange River.

Further exploration in the Kimberley region of South Africa revealed volcanic pipes filled with a hitherto unknown rock type which contained diamonds. The rock, a variety of peridotite, was named kimberlite and was recognised as the diamond source rock: this discovery formed the basis of the huge modern diamond industry. Many similar pipes have since been found in other African countries, Siberia, India and China. A closely related rock type, lamproite, is the source of Western Australian diamonds.

Diamond possesses many interesting properties in addition to its supreme hardness, lustre, and fire. Some, like its attraction to grease and blue fluorescence under X-rays, are exploited in recovering diamond from the host rock. Many diamonds also fluoresce in ultraviolet light, and the variable nature of this fluorescence provides an interesting means of identifying jewellery set with many diamonds (fig. 40).

Properties of diamond
Chemical composition: carbon
Crystal system: cubic
Hardness: 10
Specific gravity: 3·515
Refractive index: 2·417
Dispersion: 0·044

39 Red garnet crystal in a cut diamond

38 Diamond in conglomerate, from Golconda, India

40 The Murchison Snuff Box, in daylight and ultraviolet light (left). The box is set with diamonds, most of which fluoresce in ultraviolet light. It bears a portrait of Tsar Alexander II and was presented to Sir Roderick Murchison by the Tsar in 1867, in appreciation of Sir Roderick's geological work in Russia. Sir Roderick Murchison was the second director of the British Geological Survey

RUBY & SAPPHIRE

The beauty of ruby and sapphire lies in the richness and intensity of their colours. Both gems are varieties of the mineral corundum which is the hardest mineral after diamond; consequently they take a brilliant and lasting polish that adds a glittering lustre to their colours.

Pure corundum is colourless, all gem colours being caused by small amounts of chemical impurities (fig 43). Chromium gives the rich red of ruby and also causes a red fluorescence which further enhances the colour. Sapphire is the name given to all other gem corundum but is most closely associated with the blue sapphires that are coloured by iron and titanium. However, varying amounts and combinations of iron, titanium and chromium give rise to many other colours (figs 42, 43). Pinkish-orange sapphires are sometimes called 'padparadscha', a name derived from the Sinhalese word meaning lotus-colour. Improvement of colour by various forms of heat-treatment has become common in recent years.

Corundum is an aluminium oxide with trigonal crystal structure. Much ruby occurs as tabular (flat) crystals, while sapphire crystals are commonly barrel-shaped or pyramidal. Many sapphire crystals are multi-coloured, most often blue and yellow. Ruby and sapphire are strongly pleochroic, so must be cut carefully to display the best colour.

Many fascinating structures and mineral inclusions occur in ruby and sapphire, and are invaluable in distinguishing natural gems from synthetics. Slender rutile needles cause the shimmering effect known as 'silk', and when parallel to the three horizontal crystal directions may give rise to a star effect (fig 44). Chevron-shaped growth zones, liquid-filled 'feathers' and crystals of zircon and many other minerals are also common as inclusions (pp 48–49).

The Mogok area of Burma has produced fine rubies for many centuries, the best stones

41 Crystals: Burmese rubies and Kashmir sapphires

displaying a colour sometimes described as 'pigeon's blood'. A few are mined from the marble in which they formed, but most are recovered from river gravels. The gem gravels of Sri Lanka are similarly famous for an abundance of sapphires of all colours. Fine cornflower-blue sapphires occur in Kashmir pegmatites, but few are mined today. Australia is the present most prolific source of blue and golden sapphires. Basaltic rocks are the hosts of both these and the rubies and sapphires of Thailand and Kampuchea, but almost all are mined from river gravels. Fine rubies have also been discovered in Kenya, Tanzania and Zimbabwe.

Properties of corundum
Chemical composition: aluminium oxide
Crystal system: trigonal
Hardness: 9
Specific gravity: 3·96–4·05
Refractive indices: 1·76–1·78
Birefringence: 0·008–0·010

43 The many colours of corundum

42 Rare orange sapphire

44 Star rubies and sapphires

45 Ruby and sapphire fragments from gem gravels

EMERALD & AQUAMARINE

46 Beautifully formed crystals of aquamarine, heliodor, morganite and emerald

The beauty of these gems, which are varieties of the mineral beryl, lies in their superb colours. Although beryls lack the fire, high lustre and great hardness of diamond and corundum, the unique velvety green of fine emeralds places them among the most precious of gems.

As with many other gems, the colours in beryl are caused by chemical impurities. Pure beryl is a colourless beryllium aluminium silicate, but minute traces of chromium are sufficient to cause the rich green of emerald. Iron gives rise to the greenish-blues of aquamarine and the golden yellow of heliodor, whilst pink morganite and the rare red beryl are coloured by manganese. Much greenish-blue aquamarine is heated to produce the blue colour so popular in modern jewellery.

Flawless emeralds are exceedingly rare. Many emeralds are fractured and most contain mineral inclusions which, as in corundum, are invaluable in distinguishing natural gems from synthetics. Some inclusions are typical of a particular locality, such as the 'three phase' inclusions found in Colombian emeralds (fig 122). By contrast, many aquamarines, heliodors and morganites are virtually flawless, the most common inclusions being slender parallel tubes known as 'rain'.

These variations reflect the origins of the beryl varieties. Aquamarine, heliodor and morganite occur in granites and pegmatites, often as large, beautifully-formed hexagonal crystals (fig 46). Brazil is the most abundant source of aquamarine, but fine beryls are also found in Madagascar, California, the Ural Mountains and Adun Chilon in Russia and many other localities.

The finest emeralds are found around Muzo and Chivor in Colombia, where they occur in veins within dark shales and limestones (fig 47). This source was mined by

47 Emerald and calcite crystals, Colombia

the ancient Indian civilisations and was the origin of the large emeralds that flooded into Europe and Asia during the sixteenth century, after the Spanish conquest. Before this time, Egypt and Austria supplied the emeralds used by the Romans and in medieval Europe. Mica schists are the host rocks for these and many recently discovered deposits, and most emeralds from these localities contain flakes of mica. Few emeralds can match the colour of the best Colombian stones but some fine emeralds are mined at Sandawana in Zimbabwe, Kitwe in Zambia and Swat in Pakistan.

Properties of beryl
Chemical composition: beryllium aluminium silicate
Crystal system: hexagonal
Hardness: 7·5
Specific gravity: 2·63–2·91
Refractive indices: 1·568–1·602
Birefringence: 0·004–0·010

48 Fine greenish-yellow beryl

OPAL

49 Australian opal: craggy opal matrix from Queensland, an opal cameo and two doublets

Opal occurs in two distinct varieties – precious opal and common opal. Both varieties are cut as gemstones but only precious opal displays the rainbow iridescence so highly prized in jewellery from Roman times onwards.

The play of changing colours arises by the reflection and scattering of light from the minute, uniformly sized and closely packed silica spheres that make up precious opal (fig 26). This orderly arrangement is not a crystalline structure for opal is one of the few gem minerals that is non-crystalline, or only poorly so.

Common opal shows a wide range of colours and patterns but displays no iridescence because it lacks the regular fine structure of precious opal.

The body colour of precious opal varies, being pale in white opal and black, grey or brown in black opal. Fire opal

ranges from yellow to orange and red, and may show no iridescence, while water opal is clear and virtually colourless but with an internal play of colour. In matrix opal, the precious opal fills pore spaces or occurs as narrow veins in the host rock.

The name opal probably derives from 'upala', the Sanskrit word for precious stone. Although this suggests an eastern source for opal, those used by the Romans came from Dubník near Prešov in Czechoslovakia. The Aztecs mined Central American opal and some fine pieces were sent back to Europe by the Conquistadors.

The discovery of superior quality opal in Australia during the 1870s led to the decline of European production. Australia is still the principal source of black and white opal, while Mexico produces fine fire opal and water opal.

Some precious opal forms in gas cavities in volcanic rocks, as in Mexico and Czechoslovakia, but most Australian deposits

occur in sedimentary rocks. Opal contains varying amounts of water, and some material may crack if allowed to dry out too rapidly after being mined.

Opal is usually cut as cabochons, but opal veins are often thin and fragile slivers may be backed with common opal or glass to form doublets. In triplets the opal is further protected by a capping of clear quartz or plastic.

Properties of opal
Chemical composition: silica with some water
Crystal system: amorphous or only poorly crystalline
Hardness: 5·5–6·5
Specific gravity: 1·98–2·25
Refractive index: 1·43–1·47

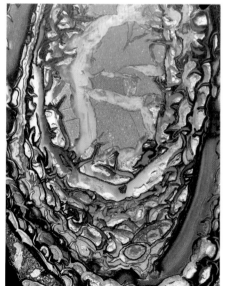

50 Opal in sandstone matrix

51 Mexican fire opals

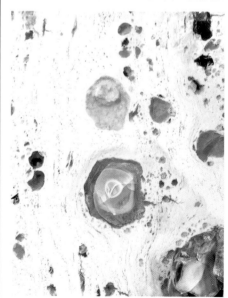

52 Fire opal in an alunite matrix

AMETHYST & CITRINE

53 Colourless and smoky quartz crystals, amethyst and citrine, milky quartz carving, star and rose quartz.

The gems described on these and the following two pages are composed of quartz, one of the most common minerals in the Earth's crust. Quartz displays a profusion of colours, patterns and optical effects unmatched by other gem minerals, ranging from the transparent colours of amethyst and citrine to the silky sheen of tiger's-eye and the intricate banding of agate. The natural abundance and infinite variety of quartz have made it the most widely used of all gem minerals.

The name quartz is usually reserved for the varieties described below, which occur as individual crystals or coarsely granular aggregates.

Colourless, transparent rock crystal is the purest form of quartz. The colours of amethyst, citrine, rose and smoky quartz are caused by chemical impurities: iron in amethyst and citrine, titanium and iron in rose quartz, and aluminium in smoky quartz. Brazil is the most important source of these varieties.

In some quartz the colour may be altered by heating, or by irradiation with X-rays or gamma rays. Natural yellow citrine is comparatively rare and most commercial citrine is amethyst turned yellow by heating.

The beauty of much quartz derives from other minerals trapped or grown within it, such as slender golden rutile crystals and tree-like metallic oxides. Some rose quartz contains abundant tiny rutile needles which cause a star effect, usually best seen when light shines through a cabochon. Asbestos fibres reflect the cat's-eyes seen in some quartz, whilst the coloured spangles in aventurine quartz are small reflecting flakes of green fuchsite mica, brown iron oxides or silvery pyrite crystals.

Tiger's-eye and hawk's-eye (fig 54) form when blue crocidolite asbestos is replaced by quartz. The asbestos breaks down, either leaving a residue of brown iron oxides as in tiger's-eye, or retaining the original blue colour, as in hawk's-eye. South Africa produces most tiger's-eye and hawk's-eye.

Faceted cuts are used for fine transparent amethyst, citrine and smoky quartz and the remaining varieties are cut as cabochons. Quartz is quite tough so that most varieties can be carved. Rock crystal has been fashioned into delicate bowls for many centuries.

Properties of quartz
Chemical composition: silica
Crystal system: trigonal
Hardness: 7
Specific gravity: 2·65
Refractive indices: 1·544–1·553
Birefringence: 0·009

54 Tiger's-eye and hawk's-eye

55 Box set with a large citrine, and a carving in cat's-eye quartz

AGATE & JASPER

56 Chrysoprase cameo

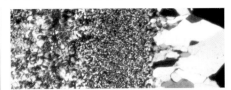

58 The structures of chalcedony and quartz (right), × 20

59 Bloodstone

Agate and jasper are the chameleons of the gem world, displaying a bewildering variety of subtle colours and patterns. Like amethyst and citrine, they are varieties of quartz, but differ in consisting of minute fibres and grains that are visible only at high magnification. The gems described here fall into two groups – chalcedony and jasper – distinguished by their internal structure.

Chalcedony, which includes all agates, cornelian and chrysoprase, forms by the build-up of thin layers of tiny quartz fibres (fig 58). This layered structure is visible as the colour banding in agate and onyx. Because of its fibrous structure, chalcedony is extremely tough and has been recognised for centuries as an excellent carving material. This toughness and colour banding are most brilliantly exploited in the classical Roman cameos (fig 2, p.2)

Pure chalcedony is a translucent grey or white, all colours and patterns arising from impurities. Iron oxides cause the browns in

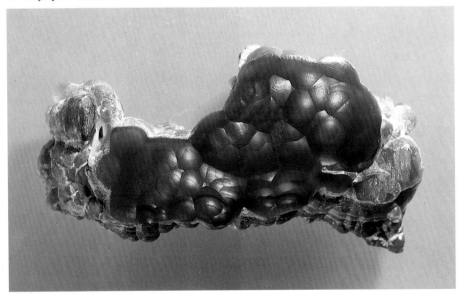

57 Fire agate from Mexico

60 Mocha stone

agates and sardonyx, and the red of cornelian. Apple-green chrysoprase is coloured by nickel (fig 56), whilst the darker greens of plasma and prase are due to countless tiny crystals of chlorite and actinolite. Bloodstone is plasma that is speckled with red jasper (fig 61).

Some moss agate contains a tangle of moss-like green minerals, but the variety known as mocha stone is patterned with iron or manganese oxides (fig 60). The iridescent colours of fire agate are produced by interference of light at thin layers of regularly spaced iron oxide crystals within the chalcedony (fig 57).

Chalcedony is porous and may be stained with a variety of metallic salts (fig 62). Natural black onyx is rare and most onyx is produced by soaking agate in sugar solution, then heating it in sulphuric acid to carbonise the sugar particles. A similar process was used by the Romans.

Jasper consists of a mass of minute, randomly arranged, interlocking quartz crystals. It is opaque and contains large amounts of colourful impurities which consist mostly of red and yellow iron oxides or green chlorite and actinolite. Jasper is used for carvings and in mosaics and inlays.

Agate and jasper occur world-wide but Brazil and Uruguay are the present most important sources of agate.

61 Frog carved in bloodstone

Properties of chalcedony
Chemical composition: silica
Crystal system: trigonal (microcrystalline)
Hardness: 6·5–7
Specific gravity: 2·6
Refractive index: 1·535 (mean)
Birefringence: rarely seen

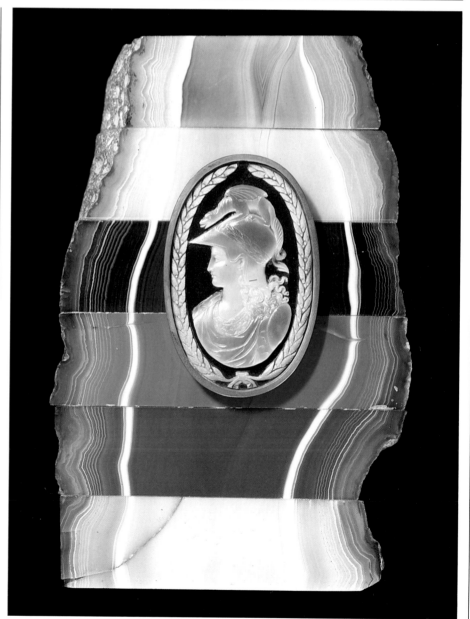

62 Sardonyx cameo resting on dyed agate slabs

TOURMALINE

Tourmaline shows the greatest colour range of any gemstone, almost any shade seemingly possible, although pink and green stones are the most popular. Some crystals are multi-coloured, with different colours occurring at either end of the crystal (fig 64), or forming a core and rim, as in 'water melon' tourmaline.

Much tourmaline occurs as beautifully formed, elongate crystals with a distinctive 'rounded triangular' shape in cross section.

Many crystals exhibit polarity: that is, the colour, electrical properties and the crystal forms are different at either end of the crystal. These fascinating variations arise from the complex crystal structure and chemistry of tourmaline.

Tourmaline is a borosilicate mineral that varies greatly in its composition. John Ruskin, the eminent Victorian thinker, wrote of tourmaline that 'the chemistry of it is more like a medieval doctor's prescription than the making of a respectable mineral'. Although most gem tourmaline is lithium-rich, there is no simple correlation between chemical composition and colour.

Tourmaline is strongly pleochroic: the deepest colour is always seen when looking down the length of the crystal. Some green and blue tourmaline appears almost black in this direction, so that it is important to orient rough material correctly when cutting gems.

Most tourmaline forms in granites and pegmatites. Famous gem localites include Brazil, Pala in California, and Sverdlovsk in Russia.

Properties of tourmaline
Chemical composition: complex borosilicate
Crystal system: trigonal
Hardness: 7–7·5
Specific gravity: 3·0–3·25
Refractive indices: 1·610–1·675
Birefringence: 0·014–0·034

63 Some of the many colours of tourmaline

64 Pink and green tourmaline crystal from California

In the past it was thought by many people that all yellow gems were topaz and that all topaz was yellow. Topaz, however, varies from pale blue and colourless to yellow, orange, brown and pink (fig 65). The pink stones so popular in Victorian jewellery were produced by heating golden-brown topaz from Ouro Preto, Brazil. Today, vivid blue topaz is produced by irradiating and then heating certain colourless material (fig 66).

Topaz is reputedly named from Topazius, the ancient Greek name for Zebirget in the Red Sea. Peridot, however, is the gem mined from this island; the stone described by Pliny as chrysolite is probably the modern topaz.

Topaz is an aluminium silicate that contains up to 20 per cent fluorine or water, its physical and optical properties varying according to the proportions of water and fluorine present. Golden-brown and pink topaz contains more water and tends to form long crystals. Such topaz is less dense and more highly refractive than the fluorine-rich colourless, pale blue and yellow topaz which occur as squat crystals.

Although topaz is the hardest silicate gem mineral, it cleaves easily along a direction parallel to the base of the crystal (fig 65).

Topaz occurs chiefly in granites and pegmatites, and in the contact zones around them. Some gem-quality crystals are huge: crystals weighing many kilograms are not uncommon. Fine golden and pink crystals from Ouro Preto, Brazil, blue crystals from the Ural Mountains and yellow topaz from Saxony grace many mineral collections.

Properties of topaz
Chemical composition: aluminium fluoro-
    silicate with some hydroxyl
Crystal system: orthorhombic
Hardness: 8
Specific gravity: 3·49–3·57
Refractive index: 1·606–1·644
Birefringence: 0·008–0·011

65 Topaz crystal and cut stones resting on the cleavage surface of a large crystal.

66 Crystal, carving and treated blue topaz

PERIDOT

The attraction of peridot rests in its colour, ideally a rich 'oily' green but ranging from pale golden-green to brownish green. The Red Sea island of Zebirget (St John's Island) was the source of peridot used by the ancient Mediterranean civilisations and is still worked sporadically to produce some of the finest peridot. The Greeks and Romans knew the island as Topazios and called this green gem topaz; peridot is a French word, possibly derived from the Arabic 'faridat', meaning gem. Today fine peridot is also mined in Burma, Norway and Arizona.

Peridot is the transparent gem variety of olivine, a magnesium iron silicate mineral which occurs in basalts and peridotite rocks. Iron causes the colour in peridot and the proportion of iron present determines the shade and depth of colour. The pale golden-green and most valuable deep green peridots contain smaller amounts of iron than the less attractive brownish-green stones.

Peridot is relatively soft and has a distinctive oily lustre. It is strongly doubly refractive so that the facet edges of a cut stone appear doubled when viewed through the stone. Many peridots contain inclusions that resemble waterlily leaves (fig 126).

In 1952 many brown stones thought to be peridots were found instead to be a borate mineral (fig 68). This newly recognised mineral was named sinhalite after its most important source, Sri Lanka, for which the Sanskrit name is Sinhala.

Properties of peridot
Chemical composition: magnesium iron silicate
Crystal system: orthorhombic
Hardness: 6·5–7
Specific gravity: 3·22–3·40
Refractive indices: 1·635–1·695
Birefringence: 0·035

68 Sinhalite

67 Fine cut peridot of 146 carats (centre) with crystals and rough mass (right) from Zebirget, and Hawaiian basalt containing olivine crystals (left)

69 The natural colour range of zircon

70 Fine zircon crystal from Norway

Although the name zircon comes from the Arabic 'zargoon' meaning vermillion or golden coloured, zircons also occur in a wide range of subtle greens and browns and are occasionally colourless (fig 69). Such stones have been used for many centuries in Indian and Sinhalese jewellery.

In western jewellery zircons are most familiar as lustrous and fiery vivid blue, golden or colourless stones which are usually cut as round brilliants. These colours are produced artificially by heating brown zircon from Thailand, Kampuchea and Vietnam. Heating in an oxygen-free atmosphere produces blue zircon (fig 71), which may then

71 Natural brown and heat-treated blue zircons.

be heated in air to give the golden colour; both processes produce some colourless material. Heat-induced colours sometimes fade on exposure to light but may be restored by careful reheating.

Zircon resembles diamond in its fine lustre and fire, so that colourless stones have been both mistakenly identified as diamonds and purposely used as diamond simulants. Zircon is easily distinguished by signs of wear and double refraction. Although zircon is moderately hard it can be very brittle, and the facet edges of cut stones are easily chipped in wear. It is also strongly doubly refractive, the facet edges appearing doubled when viewed through the stone.

Zircon contains traces of uranium or thorium which produce a distinctive absorption spectrum (fig 72 and p. 56). Radiation from these elements may gradually disrupt and transform the tetragonal crystalline structure to a 'metamict' state. Such zircons are usually green and cloudy, show only slight double refraction, and have lower refractive indices, density and hardness.

Properties of zircon
Chemical composition: zirconium silicate
Crystal system: tetragonal
Hardness: 7·5
Specific gravity: 4·6–4·7
Refractive indices: 1·923–2·015
Birefringence: 0·042–0·065

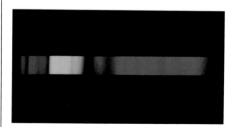

72 Absorption spectrum of zircon

GARNET

The name garnet may derive from the Latin 'granatum', meaning pomegranate, inspired by the similar red colours of the fruit flesh and of many garnets. Garnet, however, is a group name for the silicate minerals almandine, pyrope, spessartine, grossular, andradite and uvarovite, so is a far more diverse gem than its name suggests. The garnet minerals share a similar cubic crystal structure and are related in chemical composition. Gem-quality garnet occurs in many countries, and beautifully formed crystals have been prized as gems for over 5000 years.

Red almandine and pyrope are the most widely used of all garnets. Almandine cabochons and carved stones have been popular since Roman times, and much nineteenth century jewellery was set with Czechoslovakian pyrope garnets (fig 73).

74 Fine demantoid garnet

73 Jewellery set with red pyropes and almandines, and orange hessonites; pink grossular crystals in marble, and large almandine crystals

Almandine is an iron aluminium garnet and pyrope a magnesium aluminium garnet, but the iron and magnesium can replace each other and so give rise to a continuous gradation of iron magnesium aluminium garnets known as the almandine-pyrope series. This chemical variation causes a gradation in gem properties, so that two apparently similar red garnets may differ in density and refractive index. Other garnet minerals form similar series. Iron causes the brownish and purplish reds of almandine, but blood-red pyrope is coloured by traces of chromium.

Spessartine and hessonite are orange garnets. Spessartine is manganese aluminium garnet, whilst hessonite is a variety of grossular, the calcium aluminium garnet. Hessonite was the most important grossular gem until the recent discovery of brilliant green crystals at Tsavo in Kenya. Pure grossular is colourless; iron causes the orange of hessonite and vanadium colours the green Kenyan grossular.

Demantoid is a rare, vivid green variety of andradite, the calcium iron garnet (figs 74, 75). It is more fiery than diamond, but this effect may be masked by the glorious colour, which is caused by chromium impurities. Sadly, demantoid is relatively soft.

Garnets may contain distinctive inclusions, such as the rutile or hornblende needles that cause a star effect in some almandine. Much demantoid contains fibrous asbestos 'horsetails', whilst most hessonite can be identified by its granular and 'treacly' texture (fig 124).

Properties of garnet
Chemical composition: magnesium, iron or
    calcium aluminium silicates (most varieties)
Crystal system: cubic
Hardness: 6·5–7·5
Specific gravity: 3·58–4·32
Refractive index: 1·714–1·887

75 Grossular and demantoid cut gems resting on andradite crystals

76 Uvarovite crystal (centre), and green, orange and colourless grossular crystals

CHRYSOBERYL

There are three very beautiful gem varieties of chrysoberyl. The pale yellow-green stones from Brazil show an extraordinary brilliance and were popular in eighteenth century Spanish and Portugese jewellery. Some chrysoberyl contains numerous parallel, needle-like inclusions and, when cut as cabochons displays the sharpest of cat's-eyes (fig 78). This chrysoberyl variety is known simply as cat's-eye or as cymophane. The third variety is alexandrite, discovered in the Ural Mountains on the birthday of Czar Alexander II in 1830. Alexandrite is famous for its dramatic colour change, from deep green in daylight to red in tungsten light.

Chrysoberyl is a beryllium aluminium oxide, exceeded in hardness only by diamond and corundum. The yellow, green and brown colours are caused by small amounts of iron or chromium, chromium also causing the alexandrite effect. In addition to the change in colour with different lighting conditions, alexandrite is remarkably pleochroic: it appears red, orange-yellow and green in different crystal directions.

Synthetic corundum and spinel have been made as poor imitations of alexandrite

Chrysoberyl crystallises in the orthorhombic system. Simple crystals are rare, but fine trillings or twinned crystals, which appear hexagonal at first glance, are found in Brazil and the Ural Mountains (fig 79). Chrysoberyl forms in beryllium pegmatites, but most gem-quality material is mined from river gravels in Sri Lanka, southern India, Brazil and Burma.

Properties of chrysoberyl
Chemical composition: beryllium aluminium oxide
Crystal system: orthorhombic
Hardness: 8.5
Specific gravity: 3·68–3·78
Refractive index: 1·742–1·757
Birefringence: 0·009

77 Yellow chrysoberyls in Victorian filigree jewellery

79 Magnificent group of alexandrite trillings

78 Cat's-eyes

80 Faceted chrysoberyl

81 Colour variation in spinel

During medieval times, magnificent red gems known as 'Balas rubies' found their way into many royal treasuries. These stones are in fact spinels, and one of the most famous, the Black Prince's Ruby, is set in the British Imperial State Crown (fig 82). The old name is probably derived from Balascia (now Badakhshan) in Afghanistan, the supposed source of these gems.

The difference in composition between spinel and true ruby is not great: ruby is aluminium oxide and spinel is magnesium aluminium oxide. However, spinels are more variable because the magnesium can be replaced by iron, manganese or zinc, and chromium and iron may replace the aluminium. These variations give rise to a range of colours (fig 81) and cause differences in density and optical properties. Pure spinel is colourless: reds and pinks are due to small amounts of chromium, iron causes green and blue colours and zinc spinel is blue.

Spinel crystallises in the cubic system. Well-formed octahedral crystals are common (fig 83), as are flat spinel twins or macles, which resemble diamond macles in shape (fig 35). Most gem quality crystals come from thermally altered limestones that are rich in dolomite. Some are mined directly from such rocks, but most come from the richer concentrations in gravels in Sri Lanka, Burma and Brazil.

Some spinels contain planes of tiny octahedral crystals, whilst others contain parallel sets of rutile needles which give rise to a star effect in cabochon-cut stones. These spinels, like some garnets, may show both six-rayed and four-rayed stars.

Properties of spinel
Chemical composition: magnesium
    aluminium oxide
Crystal system: cubic
Hardness: 8
Specific gravity: 3·58–4·06
Refractive index: 1·714–1·750

82 The Black Prince's Ruby

83 Octahedral crystals of spinel

JADE

Jade is named from the Spanish 'piedra de hijada', a term originally used for the green stone carved by the Indian civilisations of Central America (fig 84). In Europe, the name was extended to a stone with similar properties that was used in imported Chinese carvings. It was not until 1863 that the French mineralogist Damour demonstrated that the name jade was being used for the two quite different minerals, nephrite and jadeite.

Although not particularly hard, nephrite and jadeite are tougher than steel. Consequently they have been used since neolithic times for weapons and tools, and in later ages for the most delicate carvings. This toughness stems from the structure of jade which consists of a mass of microscopic, interlocking fibres and grains (fig 14, p.7). The structure also gives rise to the dimpled 'orange peel' surface seen on older carvings: the diamond abrasives used today produce a much smoother finish.

Jadeite is a sodium aluminium silicate while nephrite is a calcium magnesium aluminium silicate containing variable amounts of iron. Nephrite is generally green to creamy-white, while jadeite is more diverse, varying from white to green, brown, orange or, rarely, lilac. Iron gives rise to most greens and browns, and manganese is thought to colour lilac jadeite. The most prized of all jades is 'imperial jade', the transparent emerald-green jadeite coloured by chromium. Much jade occurs as waterworn boulders which may develop a weathered brown outer skin. This colour variation is exploited in the jadeite archer's ring in fig 85.

Jade carving was brought to perfection by the Chinese, yet from about 200 BC nephrite had to be imported from East Turkestan. Jadeite was introduced into China from Burma much later, around 1750. Jadeite is the rarer of the jades, and Burma remains the only commercial source of jadeite. Much of the central American jadeite, which was worked from about 1500 BC until the Spanish conquest, originated in Guatemala. Today fine nephrite is mined from several sources. Spinach-green nephrite has been produced from near Irkutsk in Siberia since 1850, and the Maoris have been carving material from the South Island of New Zealand for several centuries. Taiwan and British Columbia are more recent sources.

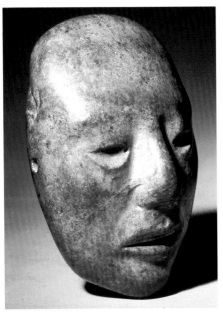

84 Maya jadeite mask

85 Jadeite ring, with nephrite boulder and vase

Properties of jadeite
Chemical composition: sodium aluminium silicate
Crystal system: monoclinic
Hardness: 6.5–7
Specific gravity: 3.3–3.5
Refractive index: 1.66 (mean)

Properties of nephrite
Chemical composition: Calcium magnesium aluminium silicate, with some iron
Crystal system: monoclinic
Hardness: 6.5
Specific gravity: 2.9–3.1
Refractive index: 1.62 (mean)

JADE

86 Carved nephrite: a tiki from New Zealand (left), a seal from British Columbia, and a Chinese vase

37

TURQUOISE

Turquoise was one of the first gems to be mined and also inspired some of the earliest known imitations. Its colour was greatly admired by the ancient Egyptians and their predecessors, who first mined turquoise in Sinai over 6000 years ago. Demand outstripped supplies very early because blue and green glazed steatite imitations have been found in graves dated at 4000 BC.

The finest turquoise occurs in Nishapur, Iran, where it has been mined for about 3000 years (fig 23, p.10). Today most turquoise is produced in the south-western United States where it is set in fine Indian jewellery. This source was known to the Aztecs who used turquoise in mosaic work on ritual masks and other ornaments (fig 87).

Turquoise is a phosphate mineral which most commonly forms as minute crystals, and occurs chiefly as veins and nodules in rocks in arid regions. The sky blue colour is due to the copper that is an essential part of its chemical composition. Much turquoise, however, also contains iron, which causes the less favoured greenish tints. Gems patterned with dark iron oxides are cut from 'turquoise matrix', which consists of turquoise and fragments of the host rock.

Turquoise is relatively soft and has a waxy lustre. As it is porous the colour may deteriorate if skin oils and cosmetics are absorbed in wear. The more porous material is friable and sometimes fades as it dries out on exposure to air. Such turquoise is usually 'colour stabilised' and made more durable by bonding with plastic resins or silica.

Properties of turquoise
Chemical composition: hydrated phosphate of copper and aluminium
Crystal system: triclinic (cryptocrystalline)
Hardness: 5–6
Specific gravity: 2.6–2.9
Refractive index: 1.62 (mean)

87 Mask of the Aztec god Quetzalcoatl

88 Turquoise vein in shale, from Victoria, Australia

LAPIS LAZULI

Lapis lazuli is named from the Persian 'lazhward' meaning blue, and its uniquely intense colour has been a source of delight for over 6000 years. For many centuries the only known deposits were those at Sar-e-Sang, in a remote mountain valley in Badakhshan, Afghanistan. From here it was exported to the ancient civilisations of Egypt and Sumer (Iraq), and later traded throughout the East and into Europe. These mines are still producing the finest quality lapis lazuli.

Lapis lazuli is a rock composed chiefly of the blue silicate mineral lazurite, together with calcite and brassy-coloured pyrite which are abundant in the poorer quality material (figs 90 and 91). The vivid blue of lazurite is caused by the sulphur that forms an essential part of its chemistry. At Sar-e-Sang the lapis lazuli occurs as a zone of lenses and veins within white marble, and grades from deep to pale blue with some violet and greenish tints.

Today lapis lazuli is also mined around Slyudyanka in Siberia and in the Ovalle Cordillera in Chile, but material from these sources usually contains much calcite.

Lapis lazuli has always been fashioned as beads and cabochons (fig 1), carved (fig 89), or used in inlays and mosaics. In medieval Europe it was crushed to produce the precious pigment ultramarine that was used in many sacred paintings and manuscript illuminations. A substitute was sought for this costly pigment and since 1828 ultramarine has been made artificially.

Properties of lapis lazuli
Composition: a rock composed mainly of lazurite, with minor amounts of calcite and pyrite. Other minerals may be present.
Hardness: 5.5
Specific gravity: 2.7–2.9
Refractive index: 1.5

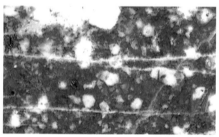

90 Fine lapis lazuli from Afghanistan

91 Siberian lapis lazuli containing much calcite

89 Carved Chinese belt-hook, with rough lapis lazuli from Badakhshan

MOONSTONE & LABRADORITE

The gems featured here are all members of the most abundant mineral group in the Earth's crust – the feldspars. Feldspar gems derive their beauty from iridescence, spangled effects or soft subtle colours (fig 93).

Feldspars are calcium, sodium or potassium aluminium silicates. They very seldom occur in a pure state but form as two distinct groups: the sodium potassium alkali feldspars and the sodium calcium plagioclase feldspars. Within each group a continuous range of compositions occurs: usually several of these compositions are intergrown within a single feldspar crystal on a fine or microscopic scale. When light is scattered or reflected by minute intergrowths and suffers interference, a beautiful soft sheen or bright iridescence may arise, as in moonstone, peristerite and some labradorite. Similar intergrowths, developed on a much larger scale, form the attractive textures of perthite.

Apart from moonstone, the alkali feldspar gems include yellow orthoclase and amazonstone. Iron impurities colour yellow orthoclase, whilst traces of lead and water cause the greenish-blue of amazonstone. Labradorite, peristerite and sunstone are plagioclase gems. The bright spangles in sunstone are reflections from tiny, flaky hematite inclusions.

Sri Lanka is the most important source of moonstone, which is mined from pegmatites and the gravels derived from them. The yellow orthoclase from Madagascar, much sunstone, and the fine amazonstone from Colorado also occur in pegmatites. Iridescent labradorite (panel above) is found chiefly in ancient crystalline rocks which formed deep in the crust. The finest labradorite comes from Labrador and Finland.

Feldspar properties
Chemical composition: calcium, sodium or potassium aluminium silicate
Crystal system: monoclinic and triclinic
Hardness: 6–6.5
Specific gravity: 2.56–2.76
Refractive indices: 1.518–1.588
Birefringence: 0.006–0.013

92 Labradorite cameo

93 Amazonstone crystals and gems, pin set with sunstone, and moonstones

Any attractive rock or mineral is a potential ornament, and many softer opaque or translucent materials are ideal for carving or fashioning into beads and other objects. A surprisingly wide range of decorative rocks and minerals has been worked through time, and a small selection appears below.

Serpentine is a rock which occurs in a great variety of colours and patterns, sometimes resembling the snakeskin from which it is named (fig 94). It is soft and easily worked, and has been used for carvings, bowls and inlay work since ancient times. Serpentine consists of the hydrated magnesium silicate minerals chrysotile, antigorite and lizardite. Lizardite was first described from the Lizard in Cornwall, the source of most British decorative serpentine. Bowenite is a translucent green serpentine that is carved extensively in China and is sometimes misleadingly called 'new jade'.

Blue John is a form of the mineral fluorite with distinctive purple and colourless or pale yellow banding. It is found at Castleton in Derbyshire where it occurs in variously patterned veins which have been given names such as Twelve Vein and Miller's Vein. Blue John has been used since Roman times, but working reached its peak in the eighteenth and nineteenth centuries when Blue John was fashioned into urns, vases and dishes (fig 96). Blue John is fragile so is usually bonded with resins for easier working and greater durability.

Malachite and *azurite* are vivid green and blue copper carbonate minerals. Malachite is often interbanded with azurite and other copper minerals such as chrysocolla (fig 95). Zaire, Zambia, Australia and Russia are sources of much fine malachite.

Rhodonite and *rhodochrosite* are pink manganese minerals. Banded rhodochrosite became a popular ornamental stone during the 1930s, after the discovery of fine material in Argentina. In 1974 an important new source was discovered at N'chwaning in Cape Province, where both banded rhodochrosite and fine transparent crystals are found. The panel at the top of the page is a detail from the lid of a polished rhodonite box.

94 Serpentine tazza

95 Malachite cameo and malachite-chrysocolla

96 Large Blue John vase

GEMS FOR COLLECTORS

97 Tanzanite

98 Taaffeite

99 Benitoite

100 Iolite

101 Andalusite

102 Fibrolite

These beautiful gems are seldom seen in jewellery but are eagerly sought by collectors of rare and curious gemstones. All are unusual in some way; prized perhaps for their extreme rarity, exceptional colour or spectacular pleochroism, or for all these qualities.

TANZANITE
Tanzanite, discovered in Tanzania in 1967, is a blue variety of the mineral zoisite. It is strongly pleochroic, displaying rich blue, magenta and yellowish-grey colours when viewed from different angles (fig 97).

TAAFFEITE
This gemstone is the first *taaffeite* ever found. It was discovered by Count Taaffe of Dublin in 1945, among gems broken out of old jewellery. Taaffeite is a very rare beryllium magnesium aluminium oxide mineral, resembling spinel in colour (fig 98).

BENITOITE
Benitoite was discovered in 1906 near the San Benito river in California, and this remains the only known locality for this barium titanium silicate mineral (fig 99).

IOLITE
Iolite is a variety of the mineral cordierite. It is famous for its pleochroism, appearing intense blue in one direction but becoming almost colourless as the stone is turned (fig 100).

ANDALUSITE & FIBROLITE
Andalusite and *fibrolite* share the same chemistry – aluminium silicate – but differ in origin and fine structure. *Andalusite* shows spectacular red and green pleochroic colours, both visible in this fine stone. *Fibrolite* is a rare variety of the mineral sillimanite. This magnificent Burmese stone shows blueish-violet and pale yellow pleochroic colours.

Fibrolite cleaves easily so large cut stones are very rare (figs 101 and 102).

SPHENE

Sphene is prized for its great lustre and fire, but is rather soft. Gem-quality crystals of this calcium titanium silicate mineral range in colour from golden browns to greens (fig 103).

KUNZITE

Kunzite is the pink variety of the mineral spodumene. It is distinctly pleochroic and cleaves easily along two crystal directions, so is difficult to cut (fig 104).

DIOPSIDE & ENSTATITE

Diopside and *enstatite* are fairly common silicate minerals. The most appealing gem varieties are the dark star diopsides and rich green chrome diopsides and chrome enstatites (fig 106).

SCAPOLITE

Scapolite of gem quality was first found in Burma, source of these cat's-eyes. Scapolite resembles feldspar in composition (fig 107).

KORNERUPINE

Kornerupine is a rare boro-silicate mineral which occurs in a range of greens and browns – this emerald-green colour is exceptional (fig 105).

103 Sphene

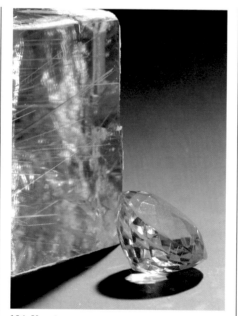

104 Kunzite

105 Kornerupine

106 Diopside and Enstatite

107 Scapolite

43

GEMS FROM PLANTS & ANIMALS

108 Centipede and insects in amber

109 Amber on a Norfolk beach

110 Jet necklaces

111 Elephant ivory carving from Japan

Plants and animals were our earliest sources of ornament, as witnessed by the carved bones and beads of ivory, amber and shell found in the remains of Palaeolithic graves and dwellings. These 'organic' gems are softer and less dense than most other gemstones, with hardnesses of 4 or less and specific gravities ranging from 1.04 (amber) to 2.78 (pearl).

Amber is a group name for fossilised tree resin, so includes many resins of differing chemical and physical properties. Trapped animals sometimes provide spectacular proof of its origin (fig 108). Most commercial amber comes from the Baltic coasts of Russia and Poland , with lesser amounts from the Dominican Republic, Sicily, Burma, North America and Mexico. Amber is less dense than most plastic and resin imitations, and will float in salty water. Baltic amber is occasionally washed up on the beaches of eastern Britain (fig 109).

Jet is fossilised wood, dark brown or black in colour and easily carved and polished. It is found as lens-shaped masses in the Upper Lias shales around Whitby in Yorkshire, and also occurs in Spain, France, Germany, Turkey, the USA and Russia. Yorkshire jet has been used since the Bronze Age, and was especially popular in Victorian mourning jewellery. Common imitations include glass, sometimes known as 'Paris jet', and the rubber derivative vulcanite.

Ivory is a name given to the teeth or modified teeth (tusks) of elephant, mammoth, walrus, hippopotamus, boar, narwhal and sperm whale. Teeth and tusks are composed mainly of the phosphate mineral hydroxyapatite and organic compounds. Ivories are identified by their structure: for example, elephant and mammoth ivory shows a pattern of intersecting curved lines in cross-section (fig 111), and walrus ivory has a distinctive coarse-grained core.

Pearls are produced by some aquatic

molluscs, especially oysters and mussels. They are secreted by the soft internal tissues of the animal around an irritant, such as a parasite or sand grain, and are built up of aragonite (calcium carbonate) layers, known as nacre. The superb iridescent lustre or 'orient' of pearl arises from the interference of light reflected from the boundaries of these thin layers. The finest pearls are produced by marine oysters of the genus *Pinctada*. Pearl mussels are freshwater animals; in Scotland and Ireland, fine pearls have been found in the species *Margaritifera margaritifera*. Some oyster and mussel species are reared in farms to produce cultured pearls. A bead or piece of body tissue is inserted into the flesh of the creature, around which the nacre is deposited to form a pearl which is harvested several years later. Cultured pearls have been produced in China for several centuries, but the modern industry was founded in Japan in the late nineteenth century.

Corals are the skeletons secreted by small sea animals called polyps. Red, pink, white and blue corals are made of calcium carbonate, but black and golden corals are formed of the horny substance conchiolin. In all corals, however, the skeletal structure is visible as a delicately striped or spotted graining. Mediterranean red and pink coral has been popular for centuries, and was once traded throughout Europe and into India and Arabia. The black and golden corals fished off Hawaii, Australia and the West Indies are much more recent discoveries.

Shells have always delighted us with their elegant shapes and patterns, but the differently coloured layers of helmet shells and giant conch shells are also exploited to produce exquisitely carved cameos (fig 114). Mother-of-pearl is the iridescent lining found in many shells, and is especially beautiful in the pearl oyster *Pinctada* (fig 113) and in abalone shells.

114 Helmet shell cameo

112 Rough and polished coral

113 Pearls and oyster shells

NOT WHAT THEY SEEM

Any attractive object is rarely in the market place for long before it is copied or imitated. Gemstones have been copied for at least 6000 years by a variety of materials which can be described as imitations, composite stones or synthetics.

Imitation gems resemble natural stones in appearance, but are usually very different in their composition and optical and physical properties. They may be man-made substances or natural minerals of similar colour to the desired gem. Glass is a favourite simulant because it can be made in almost any colour and either moulded or cut to shape. Most glass, however, is much softer than the gems that it imitates and becomes badly chipped in wear. It may also contain bubbles and display a distinctive treacly or swirly texture (fig 115). Glass is singly refractive, with a refractive index ranging between 1.5 and 1.7: no singly refractive gem minerals fall within this range.

The most recently developed imitations are the diamond simulants such as cubic zirconia and yttrium aluminium garnet (YAG), which were originally produced for use in laser and electronics research. With their high refractive indices and fire they are difficult to detect by visual tests alone, but can be distinguished from diamond by their lower reflectivity and heat conductance. Several instruments have been developed for such tests.

Composite stones have been made since Roman times. Doublets are the most common composites, consisting of two parts cemented together. Opal doublets (p.23) are usually openly described and sold as such, but doublets consisting of a coloured glass base and hard mineral top are made to deceive. Garnet-topped doublets are made to imitate gems of all colours, but the junction between garnet and glass is often easy to see, emphasised by the differences in lustre or bubbles in the adhesive (fig 117). Soudé emeralds consist of a quartz crown and

117 The junction (curved line) in a doublet

115 Bubbles and swirls in glass

116 Light leakage from a diamond (centre) and some common simulants

pavilion between which is a layer of emerald-green glass or gelatine. The composite nature of these stones is seen clearly if they are immersed in water, but detection may prove difficult when the stones are set in jewellery.

Synthetics are almost exact copies of natural gem minerals. Made under laboratory conditions, most synthetics are manufactured by melting or dissolving the appropriate mineral ingredients and colouring agents, then allowing the molten mass or solution to crystallise at strictly controlled pressures and temperatures. The resulting crystals are virtually identical in both composition and crystal structure to the natural gem mineral, so possess similar optical and physical properties.

The earliest gem-quality synthetics were the rubies produced in 1902 by Auguste Verneuil, using a flame-fusion process. Synthetic spinels and sapphires followed soon after, and this method has proved so cheap and fast that it is still used to produce most synthetic rubies, sapphires and spinels. Emeralds, however, are made by other processes, and may take nine months to crystallise from a melt: consequently synthetic emeralds are more expensive, but are still ten times cheaper than good natural stones. Today it is also possible to synthesise opal, turquoise, lapis lazuli and diamond.

Because of the difference in their values, it is essential to be able to distinguish between natural and synthetic gems. Fortunately some production methods may give rise to distinctive growth structures and inclusions, such as the curved growth zones and bubbles visible in many Verneuil-type synthetics (fig 119), or the twisted 'veils' of fluid-filled tubes in some synthetic emeralds (fig 121). Many synthetic opals display a fine scaly pattern, the 'lizard skin' effect, seen in fig 120. Flawless gems, however, pose far greater problems, so the gemmologist must resort to complex instruments and techniques such as infrared spectroscopy for the answers.

121 Wispy veils in synthetic emerald

118 Verneuil rubies and sapphire (uncut)

119 Growth zones and bubbles in Verneuil ruby.

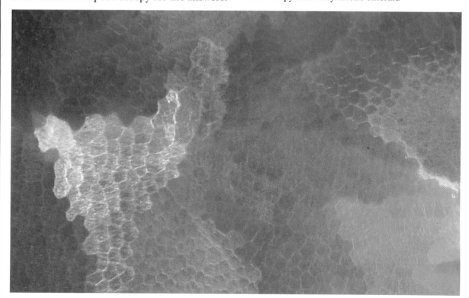

120 'Lizard skin' effect in synthetic black opal

INCLUSIONS

122 Three-phase inclusions in Colombian emerald

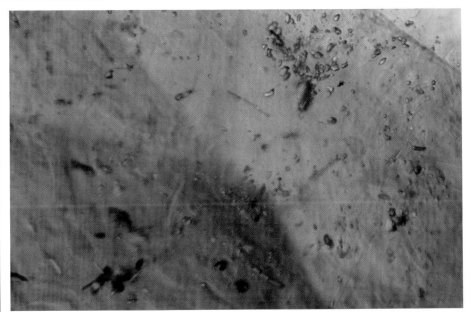

124 Rounded crystals in hessonite garnet

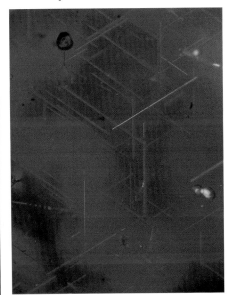

123 Rutile needles and corroded crystals in ruby

125 Rutile needles and 'feathers' in sapphire

To many people inclusions are merely flaws that reduce the value of a gemstone, but to the mineralogist and gemmologist they can reveal the gem's identity, how it formed, and even the source locality. Since the appearance of synthetic gems, they have acquired a greater importance, often providing proof of a natural or artificial origin (p.47). Most inclusions can be seen with a hand lens, but are best studied under the more powerful magnifications of a microscope, where they may appear as images of great beauty.

Many gems contain small crystals, usually of different mineral species from the host gem, which can give valuable clues to the temperatures, pressure and rock types in which they formed. For example, Colombian emeralds contain distinctive three-phase inclusions – jagged cavities containing saline liquid, a salt crystal and a gas bubble (fig 122) –which indicate that these emeralds crystallised from hot, mineralising fluids. Emeralds from many other localities contain mica flakes derived from the mica schists in which they formed. Inclusions in diamonds may provide information both about the origin of these most enigmatic of gems, and about the mantle rocks in which they formed. The ages obtained from certain mineral inclusions indicate that some diamonds formed over 3000 million years ago.

Crystal inclusions may be well formed or rounded. The distinctive internal granular texture of much hessonite garnet is formed by innumerable rounded apatite and calcite crystals (fig 124). Slender hollow tubes and needle-like crystals of rutile, hornblende and asbestos occur in many gems, often developed parallel to one or more crystal directions (figs 123 and 125); when abundant, they give rise to cat's-eye and star effects (fig 21, p.9).

Fractures and cleavages may develop in minerals as a response to stresses during their crystallisation or in later Earth movements. The 'lily-pads' seen in many peridots (fig 126) are stress fractures that develop around chromite or other crystal inclusions. Moonstones sometimes contain insect-like structures which, on closer examination, are seen to consist of small cleavage cracks (fig 127) and are quite distinct from the real insects entombed in amber (fig 108, p.44). Fractures may become partially healed during subsequent episodes of heating and alteration of the host rock: many such fractures retain pockets of trapped fluid, as in the sapphire 'feathers' in fig 125.

128 'Tiger stripe' structure in amethyst

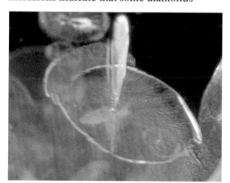

126 A 'lily pad' in peridot

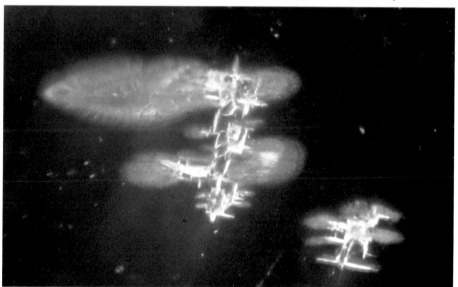

127 'Pseudo insects' in moonstone

WHERE GEMS ARE FOUND

The finding of a gem crystal or pebble can be an exciting event, especially when it leads to the discovery of a rich new gem source. Such discoveries are rare, for gem deposits occupy only a tiny proportion of the Earth's crust, their rarity stemming from the combination of physical and chemical conditions necessary for gem formation and transportation to the surface. The origins of gem minerals are as diverse as those of the rocks they occur in, and are summarised in figure 130. The numbers in the following text refer to this diagram.

Many gem minerals crystallise at high temperatures and pressures deep in the crust and underlying mantle. Diamond (9) forms at depths of 100-200 km where temperatures are about 1200°C, and from this region also come some of the red pyrope garnets and rare green chrome diopsides. Ultrabasic rocks at the crust/mantle boundary contain olivine in abundance, but only a fraction reaches the surface and only a tiny fraction of this fraction is gem-quality peridot (7). These rocks and minerals reach the surface either by uplift during mountain-building episodes (13), or in upwelling magmas (10). For example, rubies, spinels and jade formed at depth have been brought to the surface in the Himalayas, whilst zircons, garnets, rubies and sapphires are found in the basalt lavas (11) erupted from considerable depth beneath northern and southern Thailand. Once at the surface, weathering processes (14) break down the rocks and release the gem minerals, which may then be washed down-slope and concentrated by stream action in sands and gravels (15).

In the upper part of the crust pressures are low but temperatures are more variable and depend on the proximity of basaltic or granitic magmas (4 and 5). Such magmas may be sufficiently hot to convert aluminous shales to slates containing garnet, cordierite (iolite) or andalusite. Fluids arising from magmas interact with limestones to form skarns (4), which are a rich source of rare minerals and gems such as lapis lazuli, idocrase, grossular garnet and scapolite. During the final phases of crystallisation of many granites, elements such as lithium, beryllium and boron, which are relatively rare in the crust, are concentrated into the residual fluids. With falling temperatures these fluids crystallise as pegmatites (3) and form the most important source of beryl, tourmaline, spodumene and topaz. Exquisite gem-quality crystals of these minerals have been found in the pegmatites of Brazil, California, Madagascar and the Ural Mountains. Pegmatites are distinguished by the large size of their crystals. Opaque beryls and spodumenes may be several metres long, but gem-quality material is smaller, although still found in crystals weighing many kilograms.

Near the Earth's surface, magmatic fluids may interact with groundwater and cause considerable movement of material by solution and precipitation. Such fluids may leach specific metals from orebodies and redeposit them elsewhere forming secondary orebodies. The carbonates of copper – malachite and azurite – are formed in this way near copper orebodies, and turquoise (1) also is a secondary concentration of phosphate with copper and iron. Much quartz and chalcedony is deposited in fissures and cavities from silica-rich fluids; most commercial amethyst and agate is found lining and filling cavities in lavas (12).

In contrast to the gems formed from relatively rapidly moving fluids, precious opal takes shape as a collection of silica spheres under conditions of extreme stability and quiescence (2). Such conditions occur either in porous sedimentary rocks in places with a long history of crustal stability, as in Australia and Brazil, or occasionally in cavities in volcanic rocks, for example in Hungary, Czechoslovakia, Mexico and Honduras.

129 Sapphire-bearing gravel, Australia. The sapphires are derived from basaltic rock

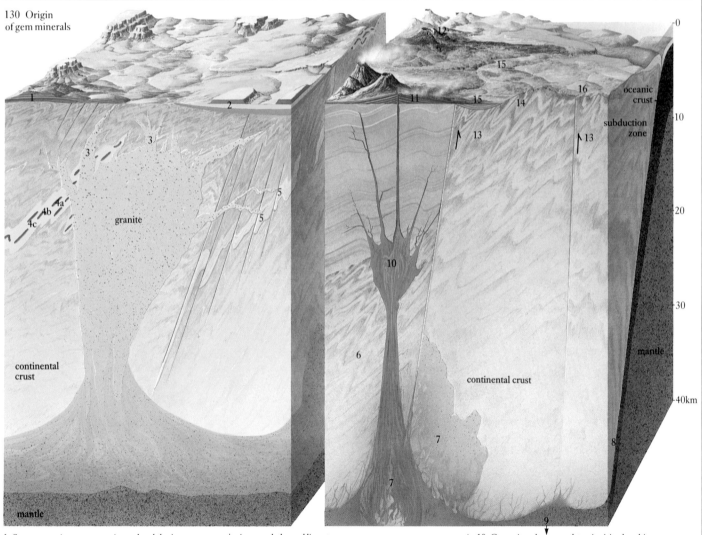

130 Origin
of gem minerals

1

2

3

3

3

4a
4b
4c

5

5

granite

continental
crust

mantle

12

15

11

15

15

14

16

oceanic
crust

subduction
zone

13

13

10

6

7

continental crust

7

8

mantle

9

0

10

20

30

40km

1 Some turquoise occurs as veins and nodules in decomposing volcanic rocks.

2 Opal in sediments forms by evaporation of silica-rich groundwater.

3 Aquamarine, tourmaline, topaz, quartz varieties, spessartine garnet, chrysoberyl, moonstone, scapolite and spodumene crystallise in pegmatites.

4 a) Ruby, sapphire, spinel and zircon, b) lapis lazuli, c) spessartine and grossular garnet, form in chemical reactions between hot granitic fluids and impure shales and limestones.

5 Emerald forms by reaction of granitic fluids with chromium-bearing rocks.

6 Ruby, sapphire, spinel, chrysoberyl and garnets form by intense alteration of aluminium-rich, muddy sediments.

7 Peridot forms in basalts and ultrabasic rocks.

8 Jadeite forms at high pressures in subduction zones.

9 Pyrope garnet and diamond form in the mantle.

10 Gem minerals are caught up in rising basaltic magma.

11 Gem minerals reach the surface in basalt lavas.

12 Much amethyst, citrine, agate and opal are deposited from silica-rich fluids and fill gas cavities in lavas.

13 Gem-bearing rocks are uplifted to the surface.

14 Weathering releases gem minerals into the soil.

15 Gem minerals accumulate in river gravels.

16 Jadeite boulders accumulate in rivers.

DIAMOND FIELDS

Diamonds are found either in pipe-like bodies of kimberlite rock, or in river and beach gravels where they accumulate after erosion of these pipes.

All diamonds are valuable, either as gemstones or in industry, so they are mined in a much more systematic and mechanised way than other gem minerals. Kimberlite pipes range from a few metres to 1·5 km in diameter and may reach depths of 3 km. All pipes are mined from open pits to about 300 metres, then by a variety of underground techniques, one of which is the block caving method shown in fig 131. Kimberlite contains on average about 25 carats (5 grams) of diamond per 100 tonnes of ore, of which only 5 carats may be gem quality.

By contrast, the Namibian beach deposits are mined in huge open pits, behind protective walls built from the sands that are removed to give access to the ancient, diamond-bearing beach terraces. The yield here is only 5 carats of diamond for every 150 tonnes of rock removed, but almost all this is of gem quality.

These minute amounts are recovered by exploiting the unique properties of diamond. Ores are first crushed and the heavy minerals, including diamond, are separated out. The heavy minerals may be passed onto a grease belt where a stream of water washes away all material except the diamonds, which are non-wettable and stick to the grease. Alternatively they are passed through an X-ray beam: the diamonds fluoresce and are diverted into a separate container.

Rough diamonds are sorted firstly into gem and industrial qualities. Gem-quality crystals are then sorted according to their size, shape, the extent and position of flaws, and colour.

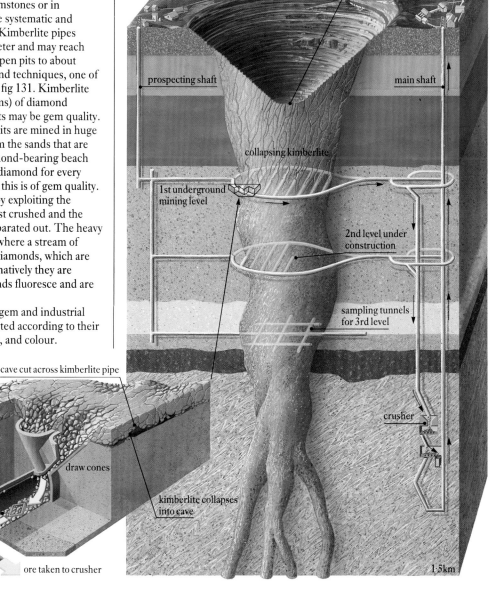

open pit mining to 300m

prospecting shaft

main shaft

collapsing kimberlite

1st underground mining level

2nd level under construction

sampling tunnels for 3rd level

crusher

cave cut across kimberlite pipe

draw cones

kimberlite collapses into cave

scraper drifts

scraper winch

ore taken to crusher

1·5km

131 Mining a kimberlite pipe

Gem gravels are among the most abundant sources of fine gems; many of the world's most famous gems were mined in the Golconda diamond fields of India or the gravels of Burma and Sri Lanka.

Gem-rich gravels form because most gem minerals are harder and more chemically resistant to weathering processes than the rocks in which they form. Gem grains either accumulate in the weathered surface layer of the parent rock, or are washed down slope and deposited in river gravels some distance away from their source. Since gem minerals are generally heavier than many common minerals, concentrations build up wherever river flow decreases in speed and volume. Flawed fragments are more readily destroyed when gem minerals are transported over long distances and in turbulent conditions, so some gravels contain a high proportion of fine-quality material.

The patchy distribution of gem material in any deposit, whether gravel or parent rock, makes a prediction of potential yield almost impossible. As many deposits are also small or in remote and difficult terrain, large-scale mechanised mining is rarely economic. Unconsolidated gravels are the most easily worked of all gem deposits, and some gem gravels have been hand-dug for centuries. At Pailin (fig 132) the gravel is washed and sorted on a simple shaking-table (centre), and the sapphires are hand-picked from the smaller residues (right foreground).

Mining in the Australian sapphire fields is more systematic and mechanised (fig 133). Boreholes are drilled first to determine the extent and yield of the gravels. After removal by large earth-moving equipment the gravel is broken up and sorted into size fractions in a trommel (rotating drum). The smaller material, which contains the sapphires, is passed onto pulsating jigs which concentrate the heavy minerals. This concentrate is finally sorted and graded by hand.

132 Gravel workings in the ruby and sapphire fields at Pailin, Kampuchea

133 Sapphire workings at Kings Plains Creek, New South Wales

GEM DEPOSITS OF THE WORLD

Exploration of our planet has revealed gem deposits in almost all countries. A few areas are rich in both the variety and quantity of gem minerals produced, examples being Minas Gerais in Brazil and Mogok in Burma. Other localities yield a single gem species of superb quality, as typified by Colombian emeralds. Most deposits are small and rapidly exhausted but a few, such as those of Burma, Sri Lanka and Afghanistan, have been in production for many centuries. The symbol ⚥ indicates deposits that are historically important but yield little or nothing today.

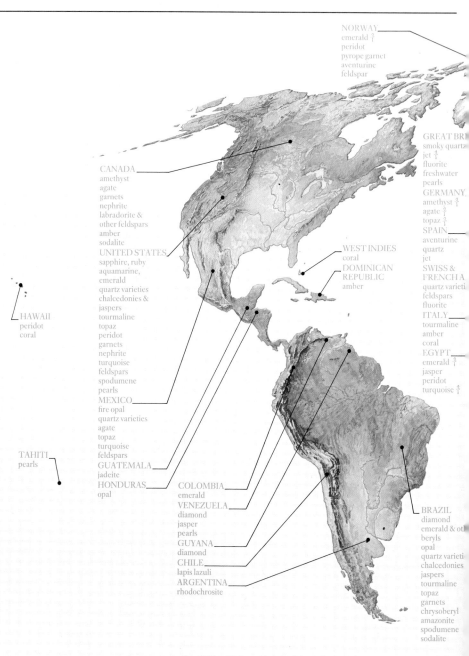

NORWAY
emerald ⚥
peridot
pyrope garnet
aventurine
feldspar

GREAT BR
smoky quartz
jet ⚥
fluorite
freshwater
pearls

GERMANY
amethyst ⚥
agate ⚥
topaz ⚥

SPAIN
aventurine
quartz
jet

SWISS &
FRENCH A
quartz varieti
feldspars
fluorite

ITALY
tourmaline
amber
coral

EGYPT
emerald ⚥
jasper
peridot
turquoise ⚥

CANADA
amethyst
agate
garnets
nephrite
labradorite &
other feldspars
amber
sodalite

UNITED STATES
sapphire, ruby
aquamarine,
emerald
quartz varieties
chalcedonies &
jaspers
tourmaline
topaz
peridot
garnets
nephrite
turquoise
feldspars
spodumene
pearls

MEXICO
fire opal
quartz varieties
agate
topaz
turquoise
feldspars

GUATEMALA
jadeite

HONDURAS
opal

HAWAII
peridot
coral

TAHITI
pearls

WEST INDIES
coral

DOMINICAN
REPUBLIC
amber

COLOMBIA
emerald

VENEZUELA
diamond
jasper
pearls

GUYANA
diamond

CHILE
lapis lazuli

ARGENTINA
rhodochrosite

BRAZIL
diamond
emerald & ot
beryls
opal
quartz varieti
chalcedonies
jaspers
tourmaline
topaz
garnets
chrysoberyl
amazonite
spodumene
sodalite

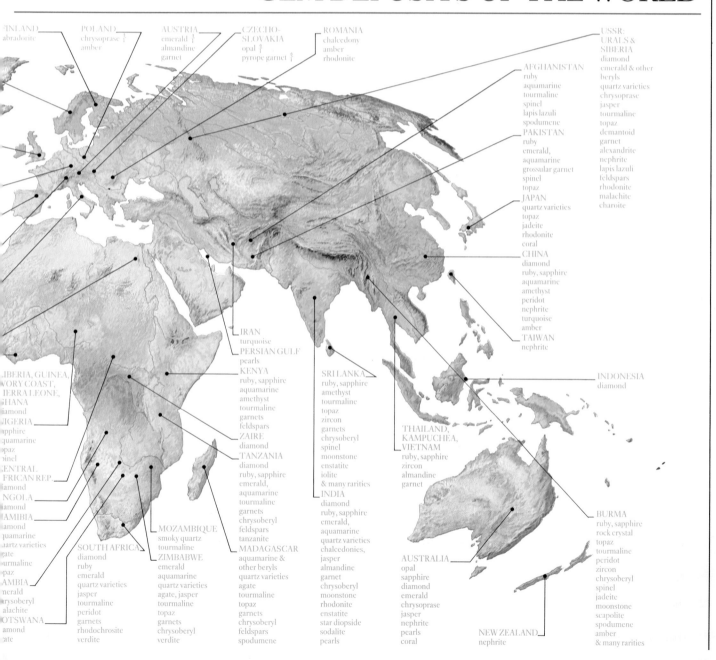

FINLAND
labradorite

POLAND
chrysoprase ?
amber

AUSTRIA
emerald ?
almandine
garnet

**CZECHO-
SLOVAKIA**
opal ?
pyrope garnet ?

ROMANIA
chalcedony
amber
rhodonite

AFGHANISTAN
ruby
aquamarine
tourmaline
spinel
lapis lazuli
spodumene

PAKISTAN
ruby
emerald,
aquamarine
grossular garnet
spinel
topaz

JAPAN
quartz varieties
topaz
jadeite
rhodonite
coral

CHINA
diamond
ruby, sapphire
aquamarine
amethyst
peridot
nephrite
turquoise
amber

TAIWAN
nephrite

**USSR:
URALS &
SIBERIA**
diamond
emerald & other
beryls
quartz varieties
chrysoprase
jasper
tourmaline
topaz
demantoid
garnet
alexandrite
nephrite
lapis lazuli
feldspars
rhodonite
malachite
charoite

IRAN
turquoise

PERSIAN GULF
pearls

KENYA
ruby, sapphire
aquamarine
amethyst
tourmaline
garnets
feldspars

ZAIRE
diamond

TANZANIA
diamond
ruby, sapphire
emerald,
aquamarine
tourmaline
garnets
chrysoberyl
feldspars
tanzanite

MOZAMBIQUE
smoky quartz
tourmaline

ZIMBABWE
emerald
aquamarine
quartz varieties
agate, jasper
tourmaline
topaz
garnets
chrysoberyl
verdite

MADAGASCAR
aquamarine &
other beryls
quartz varieties
agate
tourmaline
topaz
garnets
chrysoberyl
feldspars
spodumene

SRI LANKA
ruby, sapphire
amethyst
tourmaline
topaz
zircon
garnets
chrysoberyl
spinel
moonstone
enstatite
iolite
& many rarities

INDIA
diamond
ruby, sapphire
emerald,
aquamarine
quartz varieties
chalcedonies,
jasper
almandine
garnet
chrysoberyl
moonstone
rhodonite
enstatite
star diopside
sodalite
pearls

**THAILAND,
KAMPUCHEA,
VIETNAM**
ruby, sapphire
zircon
almandine
garnet

AUSTRALIA
opal
sapphire
diamond
emerald
chrysoprase
jasper
nephrite
pearls
coral

NEW ZEALAND
nephrite

INDONESIA
diamond

BURMA
ruby, sapphire
rock crystal
topaz
tourmaline
peridot
zircon
chrysoberyl
spinel
jadeite
moonstone
scapolite
spodumene
amber
& many rarities

**LIBERIA, GUINEA,
IVORY COAST,
SIERRA LEONE,
GHANA**
diamond

NIGERIA
sapphire
aquamarine
topaz
spinel

**CENTRAL
AFRICAN REP.**
diamond

ANGOLA
diamond

NAMIBIA
diamond
aquamarine
quartz varieties
agate
tourmaline
topaz

ZAMBIA
emerald
chrysoberyl
malachite

BOTSWANA
diamond
agate

SOUTH AFRICA
diamond
ruby
emerald
quartz varieties
jasper
tourmaline
peridot
garnets
rhodochrosite
verdite

55

WHAT IS IT?

How do you identify a gemstone, given the huge range of possibilities? Experience helps, for the more stones you see and handle, the better you are able to assess such properties as colour, lustre and density. But even the most educated guess needs confirmation, and many jewellers rely on three simple instruments to do this.

You can see many significant internal and external features of a gemstone with a *lens* if the stone is first cleaned free of dust and grease. A ×10 magnification is sufficient to reveal the quality of the cut and degree of toughness (fig 135). You will also be able to see the 'orange peel' surface on jade carvings and the uneven distribution of dye on some treated stones. A study of the inclusions may yield clues to the identity and origin of a stone: crystals and straight growth zones (fig 136) are usually found in natural gems, whereas bubbles and curved growth layers are typical of glass and some synthetics. In doubly refractive gems, the back facet edges may appear doubled when viewed through the stone (fig 137).

Many gems have a unique combination of refractive index (RI) and birefringence. These properties can be measured accurately on a standard *refractometer* (fig 139) if the gem has one flat polished surface. This surface is placed on a glass prism in the top of the refractometer and light, usually of a single yellow wavelength, is beamed into the instrument. If the gem has a lower RI than the prism glass, some of this light is refracted out through the gem and the remainder is reflected back into the refractometer. When you look into the eyepiece, the junction between reflected and refracted light appears as one or two shadow edges, depending on whether the gem is singly or doubly refractive. The position of the shadow edges depends on the refractivity of the gem, so they can be read off against a scale to give the RI of the gem, within the range of 1.3 to 1.8.

The small *spectroscope* is useful in distinguishing gems and imitations of similar colours. Light entering the instrument through a narrow slit is separated into its spectrum of colours by glass prisms or a diffraction grating. If a gem is placed between a strong light source and the slit, dark bands

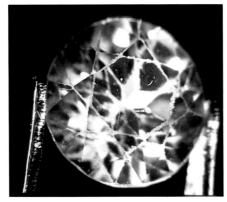

135 Badly worn zircon facets.

may appear in the spectrum where these light wavelengths are absorbed within the stone. The wavelengths absorbed vary according to the colouring element, so that the absorption spectra of gems of apparently similar colours may be very different (fig 138). This test can be used on cut stones and rough material.

137 Double refraction in sinhalite.

136 Growth zones in sapphire.

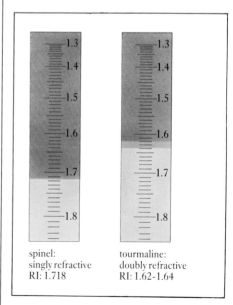

ruby: coloured by chromium

almandine garnet: coloured by iron

red glass: coloured by selenium

138 Spectroscope in use, and absorption spectra of three red stones

139 Refractometer in use, and views down the eye-piece

spinel:
singly refractive
RI: 1.718

tourmaline:
doubly refractive
RI: 1.62-1.64

SOME FAMOUS GEMS

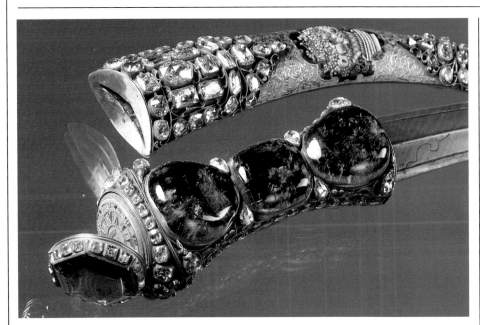

140 Dagger

142 Dresden Green Diamond

141 The Timur Ruby

Dagger (fig 140)
Topkapi Palace Museum, Instanbul
The Topkapi Palace Treasury is renowned
for its magnificent Colombian emeralds. The
hilt of this eighteenth century dagger is set
with three emeralds and surmounted by an
emerald slice which covers a small watch.
The gold sheath is decorated with diamonds
and enamelled flowers.

The Timur Ruby (fig 141)
*Private collection of Her Majesty Queen
Elizabeth II*
The huge central stone of this necklace is in
fact a red spinel, weighing 352·5 carats. A
magnificent gem in its own right, the Timur
Ruby is made even more fascinating by
inscriptions of the names of former royal
owners, which include Timur (Tamerlane)
and several Mughal emperors.

Dresden Green Diamond (fig 142)
Grünes Gewölbe, Dresden
This diamond, at 41 carats, is the largest-known green diamond and is among the rarest of gems. It was bought by Frederick Augustus II of Saxony in 1743 and is probably of Indian origin.

Koh-i-Noor Diamond (fig 143)
British Crown Jewels, Tower of London
A wealth of legend has accumulated around this, perhaps the most famous of all Indian diamonds. During a turbulent history the Koh-i-Noor passed rapidly from owner to owner – Indian, Mughal and Persian. It was presented to Queen Victoria in 1850 and was recut as a brilliant in 1852, reducing the weight from 186 carats to 108·93 carats.

The Canning Jewel (fig 145)
Victoria and Albert Museum, London
A large baroque pearl forms the torso of a merman in this Renaissance pendant, which was made in about 1570. The jewel is said to have been given to a Mughal emperor by a Medici prince, and was brought from India in 1862 by Charles John, 2nd Viscount Canning. The larger rubies and pearl drop were added in India

Hope Diamond (fig 144)
Smithsonian Institution, Washington DC.
This famous diamond is probably part of the Great Blue diamond brought back from India by Jean-Baptiste Tavernier, the great French merchant and traveller. He sold it to Louis XIV who had the gem recut, reducing the weight from 112 carats to 68·7 carats. It was stolen during the French Revolution and again recut. In 1830 it reappeared in London, now weighing 45·5 carats, and was bought by the banker Henry Hope. The diamond changed owners several more times before Harry Winston presented it to the Smithsonian Institution

143 Koh-i-Noor Diamond

145 The Canning Jewel

144 Hope Diamond

INDEX

British Library CIP Data
Gemstones
Precious stones
553.8 QE392

Authors: Christine Woodward
    Dr Roger Harding
Photographer: Frank Greenaway
Artist: Gary Hincks
Designer: David Robinson
Typesetting:
    Cambridge Photosetting Services,
    England
Printing & binding:
    Amilcare Pizzi spa. Milan

Other picture sources:
Figs 1, 2, 4, 84, 87 reproduced
    by permission of the Trustees of
    the British Museum.
Fig 3 Novosti Press Agency
Fig 5 Chaumet Ltd
Figs 10, 25, 82, 143 reproduced
    with the permission of the
    Controller of Her Majesty's
    Stationery Office
Figs 31, 32, 33 De Beers
    Consolidated Mines Ltd
Figs 65, 117, 121–129, 132, 133,
    135 E Alan Jobbins
Figs 111, 145 by courtesy of the
    Board of Trustees of the Victoria
    and Albert Museum
Figs 115, 119 Clive Burch
Figs 120, 136 Cassandra Goad
Fig 140 Ernst A Heiniger
Fig 141 reproduced by gracious
    permission of Her Majesty
    the Queen
Fig 142 Claus Hansmann
Fig 144 and inside back cover
    Smithsonian Institution

We are grateful to Mrs E Stern
and R Keith Mitchell for lending
items for figs 12, 61, 98 and 112,
and to H E K Allen for assistance
with fig 131.

© British Museum
    (Natural History) 1987

First published 1987
British Museum (Natural History)
Cromwell Road
London SW7 5BD

ISBN 0 565 01011 5 paperback